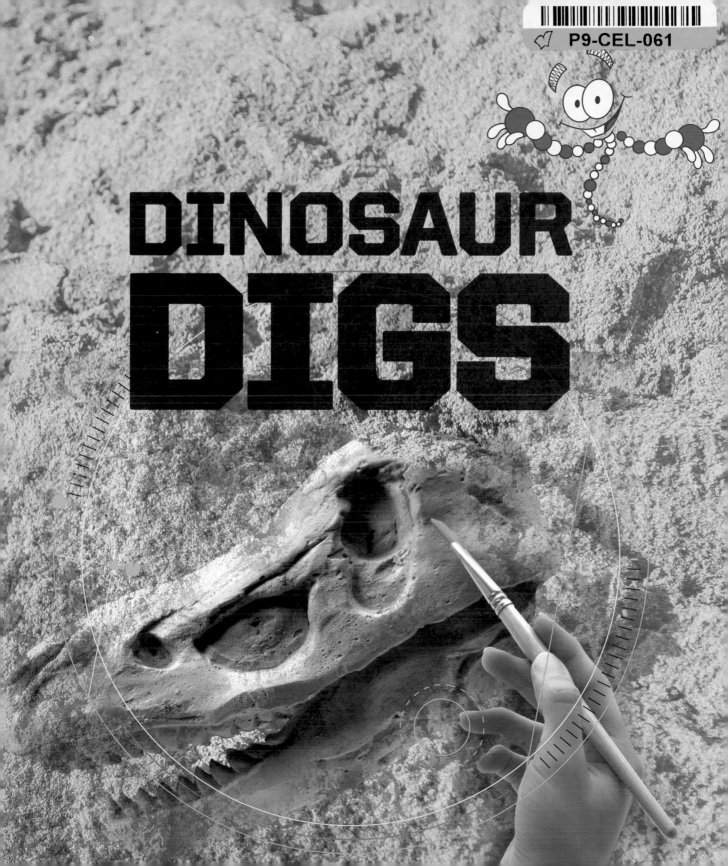

DINOSAUR DIGS

Photos ©: 1 center: Scholastic Inc.; 1 hand: Zenobillis/Shutterstock; 4 top: Ton Bangkeaw/Shutterstock; 4 bottom left: Pecold/Shutterstock; 4 bottom right: Petr Bonek/Shutterstock; 6 top: bingokid/iStockphoto; 8 left: José Antonio Peñas/Science Source; 8 right: Larissa Pereira/Shutterstock; 10 top: Mark1260423/Shutterstock; 10 top circle: Sunwand24/Shutterstock; 10 bottom left: Michael Fiedler/Shutterstock; 10 bottom right: Pornprapa Korprasert/Shutterstock; 12 top: Dreamframer/iStockphoto; 12 center: Photomontage/Shutterstock; 12 bottom: Bjoern Wylezich/Shutterstock; 13 top: Breck P. Kent/Shutterstock; 13 bottom: Alex Coan/Shutterstock; 14 top left: The Natural History Museum/Alamy Stock Photo; 14 top right: George W. Bailey/Shutterstock; 14 center left: Pictorial Press Ltd/Alamy Stock Photo; 14 center right: The Natural History Museum/Alamy Stock Photo; 14 bottom: cowardlion/Shutterstock; 16 bottom right: BigWorldPhotographic/Shutterstock; 20 center: Dinoton/Shutterstock; 22 top: Wlad74/Shutterstock; 22 center: Edgloris Marys/Shutterstock; 24 center: Yibo Wang/Shutterstock; 24 bottom: gorosan/Shutterstock; 26 top: Yannick Martinez/Shutterstock; 26 center: Rattana/Shutterstock; 28 center: David Herraez Calzada/Shutterstock; 29 top left: Potapov Alexander/Shutterstock; 30, 31 corprolites: Scholastic Inc.; 30 ruler: Christopher Beahan/Shutterstock; 31 bottom left: The National Library of Wales/Wikimedia; 32: Puwadol Jaturawutthichai/Shutterstock; 34 top: History and Art Collection/Alamy Stock Photo; 34 bottom: The Granger Collection; 36 top left: paleontologist natural/Shutterstock; 36 top right: Sanya Bu/Shutterstock; 36 compass: valzan/Shutterstock; 36 tape measure: littleman/Shutterstock; 36 marker: Salamahin/Shutterstock; 36 others: Scholastic Inc.; 37 bag: rainbow rays/Shutterstock; 38 top: benedek/iStockphoto; 38 bottom: bryngelson/iStockphoto; 40 top: gorosan/Shutterstock; 40 micropaleontology: Sergey/Shutterstock; 40 paleobotany: Adamantios/Wikimedia; 40 paleoecology: Fortgens Photography/Shutterstock; 40 paleoichnology: Dreamframer/iStockphoto; 40 taphonomy: lorenza62/Shutterstock; 44 top: GL Archive/Alamy Stock Photo; 44 bottom: Courtesy University of Kansas; 47 left: mg7/iStockphoto; 47 brush: Scholastic Inc.; 48: LeventKonuk/Getty Images.

Note to the reader: Since no photographs exist from prehistoric times, all dinosaur images are from Jurassic World archives.

Written by Marilyn Easton

Designed by Mabel Zorzano

ISBN 978-1-338-57173-8

10 9 8 7 6 5 4 3 2 1   19 20 21 22 23

Printed in China 163

First edition September 2019

TABLE OF CONTENTS

What Are Fossils?

Fossils are impressions from the past, left behind by plants, animals, and other organisms. These impressions were preserved by minerals, such as those in sand and mud, that hardened over a long period of time and maintained the shape of the item left behind. Each fossil holds information about the animal or plant that once existed.

We most commonly think of dinosaur fossils as skeletons that appear in museums. But there are many different types of dinosaur fossils, including skin, footprints, eggs, and even poop. Everything we know about dinosaurs comes from fossils.

270°

225°

180°

ONLY AT JURASSIC WORLD

◀ Without fossils, Jurassic World would not have existed. The foundation for Jurassic World science came from a fossil preserved in amber.

◀ Sir Benjamin Lockwood, John Hammond's partner in creating Jurassic Park, owned many fossilized dinosaur bones and displayed them in the library of his estate. One of Lockwood's most complete specimens was this Triceratops.

◀ One of the many skulls in Lockwood's collection.

Fossils Rock

Most fossils are found in layers of sedimentary rock. Three-quarters of the surface of the Earth is covered in this type of rock. That's a lot of potential fossil discoveries!

When a dinosaur fossil is discovered, scientists who study them—called paleontologists—can determine when that dinosaur lived based on its placement in rock layer. The oldest fossils are in the lowest layer of the rock, and the younger fossils occur near the uppermost layers. By studying which organisms are found within each rock layer, also called a stratum, scientists can map out a timeline for how and when a dinosaur first appeared in relation to other creatures.

Dinosaurs lived during a time called the Mesozoic Era. It started about 250 million years ago and ended about 65 million years ago. The Mesozoic Era is made up of three periods—the Triassic, Jurassic, and Cretaceous.

Dinosaurs weren't the only creatures that lived during the Mesozoic Era. New species of fish, plants, insects, mammals, and reptiles also lived at that time.

MESOZOIC ERA

CRETACEOUS PERIOD
145–65 million years ago. Dinosaurs like the *Tyrannosaurus rex*, Velociraptor, Ankylosaurus, and Triceratops roamed the land.

JURASSIC PERIOD
199–145 million years ago. This was the golden age for dinosaurs. Gigantic herbivores like the Apatosaurus, Stegosaurus, and others lived during this period.

TRIASSIC PERIOD
251–199 million years ago. The first dinosaurs appeared toward the end of this period. Most of them were small, quick meat eaters that walked on hind legs.

ONLY AT JURASSIC WORLD

◀ A Stegosaurus, which first lived during the late Jurassic Period, is pictured here in the famed Gyrosphere valley of Jurassic World.

Shown here during the volcanic eruption on Isla Nublar, this Baryonyx's ancestors roamed the Earth during the early Cretaceous period. ▼

The Late Cretaceous Period had many carnivores (meat eaters) like this Carnotaurus from Jurassic World. ▼

The time immediately before dinosaurs existed is called the Paleozoic Era.

Fossil Formation

Not all creatures leave behind fossils. In fact, most don't! This is because the conditions needed for fossils to form are very specific. For example, when a dinosaur died, its bones were preserved only if it was buried very quickly. This quick burial usually was a result of a mudslide or of having been stuck in tar or frozen in ice. If the dinosaur was not buried rapidly, another animal could crush its bones or carry them away. And if bones were only partially buried or exposed to the air, they would decompose instead of fossilizing, since oxygen speeds decomposition.

Over millions of years, the quickly buried bones become buried deeper and deeper under layers of dirt and sand that eventually become rock. This is when a fossil forms. Then, millions of years later, the plates beneath the earth's top layer might shift, causing the fossil to move closer to the surface until someone discovers it.

This dinosaur died in a river, and its body was buried quickly by sediment.

Over time, more and more dirt covered its body. Eventually, everything but the bones decomposed, and the dirt became rock.

Millions of years later, after the earth moved and rock eroded, the bones are uncovered by a paleontologist.

The La Brea Tar Pits in present-day Los Angeles, California, provided quick burials when mastodons, saber-toothed cats, and large ground sloths became trapped and covered in tar during the Pleistocene Era. The tar helped preserve their remains.

▲ When Jurassic World was in operation, Owen Grady worked as an Animal Behaviorist and trained Velociraptors. Owen is seen here next to the skeleton of a fallen dinosaur which, if it got buried by silt from the riverbank, could eventually become a fossil.

Ice, Tar, and Amber

Not all fossils are formed by being buried deep in the earth. Some are formed when a plant or animal became trapped in tar, ice, peat, or plant resin (which is similar to tree sap, and hardens into amber). These fossils are unique in several ways. First, they contain the entire specimen rather than just pieces of a specimen. Second, these fossils contain the exact organism as it was preserved millions of years ago—not just its bones. This means that even its last meal may still be inside its stomach!

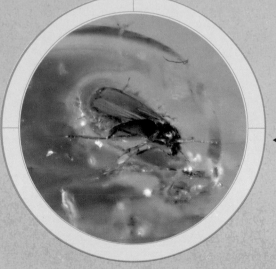

◄ This mosquito was preserved in amber.

◄ In Jurassic World, the preserved fossil of a mosquito trapped in amber gave scientists the missing information they needed to create a dinosaur. The mosquito had bitten a dinosaur, and the dinosaur's blood was still inside the mosquito when paleontologists uncovered the fossil. The blood provided the dinosaur's genetic information, or DNA.

Preserved fossils ► were so essential to Jurassic World that Dr. Wu had a wall of specimens.

A wooly mammoth was discovered preserved inside ice in Siberia, Russia.

◄ This image from the La Brea Tar Pits in Los Angeles, California, shows how now-extinct animals have been preserved.

◄ Sir Benjamin Lockwood and John Hammond had matching walking sticks topped with mosquitos fossilized in amber.

Types of Fossils

Fossils form under a variety of conditions, and they can range from a footprint to an entire organism. They can show us what a creature looked like, or they may simply provide a glimpse into its eating habits or other behaviors. No matter what their size, each fossil tells a unique story.

Petrified Fossils

Petrified fossils are items like bones that have turned to stone. They form when minerals replace part or all of an organism as its body dissolves.

Preserved Remains

Remains of prehistoric organisms might be preserved if an organism becomes trapped in amber (a sticky tree resin that has hardened), tar, or ice. Unlike the other types of fossils, preserved remains are actual, nonpetrified parts of the animals or plants to which they belonged.

Molds and Casts

A mold forms when a part of a dinosaur, like a foot or piece of skin, is pressed into soft sediment and then dissolves over time, leaving behind an impression of its shape. These fossils are also known as impressions.

A natural cast forms when minerals and sediment fill a mold and then harden over time. A cast is the opposite of the mold in which it formed: it is a 3-D replica of an organism created from a mold that filled with minerals.

Paleontologists also create casts to study fossils by filling molds with a synthetic material like latex rubber or plaster.

Trace Fossils

Trace fossils preserve records of an animal's activity instead of parts of its body. Examples of trace fossils include footprints, animal burrows, trails, and poop. Trace fossils can be petrified fossils, molds, or casts.

Dino Firsts

Iguanodon ▶

Gideon Mantell & Mary Ann Mantell Discovered the First Fossils Identified as Dinosaurs

Gideon lived: Feb. 3, 1790–Nov. 10, 1852

Birthplace: Lewes, England

Mary lived: 1799–1847 or 1795–c. 1855

Birthplace: England

Major Discovery: In 1822, Mary Ann Mantell found teeth that looked like they belonged to an iguana, except that they were much larger. She shared her findings with her husband, who eventually named the creature "Iguanodon," which means "iguana tooth." Gideon shared his findings with other paleontologists, including Richard Owen.

Other accomplishments: Gideon named Hylaeosaurus, Pelorosaurus, and Regnosaurus.

Richard Owen, The Father of Dinosaurs

Jul. 20, 1804–Dec. 18, 1892

Birthplace: Lancaster, England

Major Discovery: In 1842, after studying bones like the ones found by Gideon and Mary Mantell, Owen determined that they were from animals that differed from existing creatures. He named the older animals "Dinosauria," which means "terrible reptile" or "fearfully great reptile." This is where the word "dinosaur" comes from.

Other accomplishments: In 1881, he started the Natural History Museum in London.

The Natural History Museum in London.
▼

JURASSIC WORLD PROFILE:
JOHN HAMMOND

Originally from Scotland, John Hammond was the CEO of InGen when the first dinosaurs came to life at Jurassic Park. Sparing no expense, he founded his idealistic vision for Jurassic Park on the goal of "captur[ing] the imagination of the entire planet." Despite investor interests, Hammond did not want to charge a high price for entry to Jurassic Park; he believed that "everyone in the world has the right to enjoy these animals." Unfortunately, his dream was thwarted by a greedy employee who caused havoc before the park ever opened to the public. But his foundational work lived on, providing research for the next generation to enjoy Jurassic World.

▲ Hammond insisted on being present for the birth of every dinosaur.

"How could we stand in the light of discovery and not act?"
—John Hammond

"Our scientists have done things which nobody's ever done before." —John Hammond

What Can Fossils Tell Us?

Fossils are very important because they teach us about Earth's history. By studying where an organism is found in rock layers, scientists can determine when the first simple life forms appeared on Earth, when plants and trees first emerged, and when animals and people appeared. By comparing fossils from different time periods, scientists can also observe how organisms have changed over the years.

Dating Fossils

One method that scientists use to see how old fossils are involves the chemicals potassium and argon. Here's how it works: All fossils contain both of these chemicals. As the fossils age, though, the potassium inside them turns to argon. This means that older fossils contain more argon. Sometimes paleontologists use another method, called carbon-14 dating, for organic materials (living things). Knowing a fossil's age allows paleontologists to paint a clearer picture of its origin.

PANGEA

▲
Flowering plants emerged during the Cretaceous period.

During the Mesozoic Era, all the land on Earth was joined in one huge continent called Pangea. Two hundred million years ago, Pangea split into the continents we know today. When Pangea broke apart, dinosaurs in different land areas became separated. That's why paleontologists have discovered fossils from the same types of dinosaurs on different present-day continents.

Tyrannosaurus rex fossils have been found ▶ in America, Canada, and Mongolia.

◀ Stegosaurus fossils have been found in America, Portugal, and Madagascar.

What Can Fossils Tell Us about Dinosaurs?

Fossils help us understand extinct animals like dinosaurs. By studying individual dinosaur fossils, scientists can learn a lot of information. This includes what dinosaurs looked like, what other animals they spent time with, what they ate and what ate them, what kind of parents they were, how they grew, and more. Everything we know about dinosaurs comes from the fossils left behind.

Dinosaur skeletons might be the most spectacular of all fossils. These enormous remains help us understand how big dinosaurs really were! They bring the past to life in a way that no picture could ever match, and they show the variety of differences among dinosaurs. Paleontologists have identified approximately 700 different dinosaur species from fossils.

If a dinosaur skeleton is discovered with other bones from the same type of dinosaur, for example, paleontologists might conclude that they traveled together in herds. If a bone is found with a tooth mark in it, paleontologists can match the mark with another fossilized tooth and see which creature attacked it. If the bone appears to have healed from the wound, it may reveal that the dinosaur was able to defend itself.

Stegosaurus ▶

Triceratops ▶

ONLY AT
JURASSIC WORLD

Fossils can paint a picture of what a dinosaur might have looked like, but to re-create the animals in Jurassic World, scientists needed DNA. Scientists at Jurassic World were not able to bring back a 100 percent complete genuine dinosaur DNA strand, so they filled gaps with frog DNA. As a result, the dinosaurs at Jurassic World may not have looked exactly like what dinosaurs did millions of years ago.

This machine held the DNA for Jurassic World dinosaurs like Velociraptor and *Tyrannosaurus rex.*

VELOCIRAPTOR

TYRANOSAUR

ALLIMIMUS

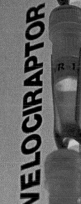

◀ Without fossils, this Ankylosaurus would not have been able to roam Jurassic World's Gyrosphere Valley.

◀ *T. rex*

Velociraptor Fossils

First discovered: August 1923

Discovered by: Peter Kaisen

Location: Gobi Desert, Mongolia

Contents of discovery: Crushed skull and toe claw

Named by: Henry F. Osborn

Name meaning: *Velociraptor* means "swift thief"

The serrated, knife-sharp teeth of the Velociraptor suggest this dinosaur was a meat eater that used its teeth to rip flesh.

◄ Velociraptor fossils have been found near fossils of eggs, suggesting that they cared for their young by watching over their nests.

The skull of the Velociraptor has a wide scleral ring. This suggests that Velociraptors hunted at night. The wide scleral ring allowed more light to enter the eye when it was dark.

◀ Dr. Ellie Sattler and Dr. Alan Grant witnessed a Velociraptor egg hatching at Jurassic Park.

Prehistoric Velociraptors weighed about as much as the modern turkey. Jurassic World scientists made adjustments to the Velociraptor DNA to make them larger and more impressive to park crowds. ▼

◀ Velociraptors had one large, sickle-like claw on each hand that was longer than the others and razor-sharp.

Dinosaur Skulls

The size and shape of a dinosaur skull can reveal a lot. Since skulls also include eye sockets, jaws, teeth, and markers of other sensory functions, scientists can uncover a lot of information from a good specimen. By comparing skull and body size with animals living today, they have determined that most dinosaurs had a brain similar to that of crocodiles or birds.

Skulls can also reveal information about a dinosaur's behavior. If the part of the skull that holds the eyes, called the scleral ring, is wide, it suggests that the animal is nocturnal. This is because the wider space allowed for more light to enter the eye when it was dark.

Until 2004, only dinosaur skull bones themselves had been discovered. Then a cast of a skull was discovered on the beach, and it contained microscopic traces of the dinosaur's brain tissue and blood vessels. This 133-million-year-old specimen expanded the realm of possible tissues that can be preserved in the fossil record.

The smallest skull ever discovered was that of a juvenile Diplodocus. It was 9 inches long.

The largest skull ever discovered was that of a Torosaurus. It was 8 feet long.

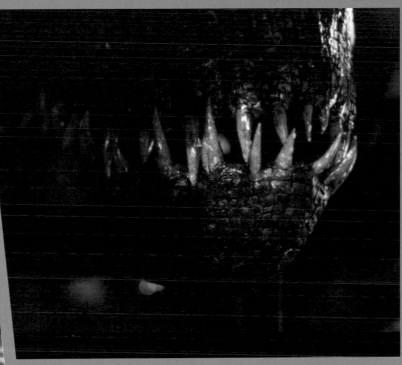

◄ The razor-sharp teeth of the Indoraptor, a hybrid created by Dr. Wu, were a clear sign that it was a carnivore.

◄ This *Tyrannosaurus rex* skull from Benjamin Lockwood's collection showed that the animal had a strong jaw, perfect for attacking prey.

Pteranodon Fossils

Fossilized skulls of Pteranodons don't have any teeth! This suggests that their diets were similar to those of birds, who also lack teeth.

First discovered: May 1876

Discovered by: Samuel Williston and B.F. Mudge

Location: Kansas, United States

Contents of discovery: Skull

Named by: Othniel C. Marsh

Name meaning: *Pteranodon* means "toothless wing"

Bite marks on a Pteranodon wing fossil have been matched to prehistoric shark teeth. This suggests to scientists that Pteranodons hunted for food while traveling over water.

Pteranodons are not actually considered dinosaurs. They belonged to a group of flying reptiles called Pterosaurs. They lived between 83 million and 70 million years ago during the late Cretaceous Period. Much like giant pelicans, Pteranodons were fierce meat eaters who hunted mostly over ocean waters. When a Pteranodon spotted prey below the water's surface, it swooped down and scooped it into its massive beak. Pteranodons had large eyes to help them with this fast-paced task.

◄ A discovery in 2008 revealed that Pteranodon eggs were soft, simil to present-day snake eggs. It als revealed that the eggs were laid nests.

Catch Me If You Can

Although they were large compared to animals today, Pteranodons were tiny compared to many carnivores of their time. They couldn't have fought off large, hungry predators. Thanks to their flight skills, though, they didn't need to! Pteranodons could glide for long distances without landing. They could flap their huge wings for an extra burst of speed if needed. Mostly, though, they rode the oceanic air currents, relaxed and safe from the many dangers found on land.

This Pteranodon showed off its impressive wingspan to guests at Jurassic World. A Pteranodon wingspan could reach up to 40 feet long.

▼

◄ An up-close look of a Pteranodon's toothless bill.

Footprints

Footprints are a type of trace fossil that reveal clues about the behavior of a dinosaur. This kind of fossil can help determine whether an animal walked on two or four feet, the length of its stride, and how quickly it moved. If an adult footprint and a juvenile footprint are near one another, that type of dinosaur may have traveled with its young. Footprints also reveal whether animals traveled in herds, like some herbivores, or traveled alone, like some carnivores.

Skin Impressions

Skin impressions are another type of trace fossil that reveal what a dinosaur may have looked like. They can help determine whether dinosaur skin was bumpy, smooth, or covered in feathers. Feathers and fossilized skin can also reveal what color a dinosaur might have been.

Scientists can confirm that a Carnotaurus had bumpy, scaly skin, thanks to an impression discovered with fossilized bones.

A fossilized Nodosaurus was discovered with skin intact. Chemical tests revealed that this dinosaur had reddish skin.

◄ Carnotaurus

One of the largest dinosaur footprints ever discovered was in Australia. It measured more than 5.5 feet and was from a Sauropod.

The smallest dinosaur footprint ever discovered was in the United Kingdom. It is 165 million years old and 0.7 inches long.

◀ Prehistoric Velociraptor fossils have recently revealed that they had feathers. Before this discovery, Jurassic World scientists were tasked with creating more thrilling, reptilian-looking dinosaurs with more teeth to deliver thrills to park guests.

◀ Tracks from *Indominus rex* would reveal that it was able to run very quickly.

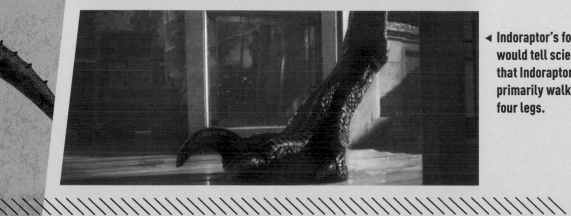

◀ Indoraptor's footprint would tell scientists that Indoraptor primarily walked on four legs.

Triceratops Fossils

First discovered: 1887

Discovered by: George Cannon

Location: Denver, Colorado, United States

Contents of discovery: Two horns and partial skull

Named by: Othniel C. Marsh

Name meaning: *Triceratops* means "three-horned face"

Triceratops had a beak that could grasp plants and tear them from the ground.

The unique skull of the Triceratops has three horns, which scientists believe may have been used for defense. Each horn was up to 3 feet long.

Triceratops had up to 800 teeth that were perfect for grinding up plants.

Triceratops lived about 67 million to 65 million years ago, during the late Cretaceous Period. This creature was twice as big as a modern-day rhinoceros. Despite its bulk, though, Triceratops wasn't usually dangerous. This herbivore roamed the land, grazing on grass and tasty leaves as it traveled. Though many other horned dinosaurs are known to have lived in herds, Triceratops fossils are usually found alone, suggesting that they may have spent much of their time by themselves. If a large carnivore attacked, though, watch out! Triceratops was big and strong, and it didn't hesitate to defend itself with its strong tail, clawed hooves, and wicked horns.

T. rex vs. Triceratops

Who would win a one-on-one battle between a *T. rex* and a Triceratops? It's hard to know for sure—it's likely that a *T. rex*. would only have preyed on younger, smaller Triceratops, not full-grown ones. But scientists have found Triceratops bones that show signs of damage from *T. rex* teeth, but which appear to have healed fully. This shows that at least some Triceratops survived encounters with *T. rex*!

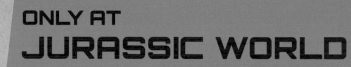

At first, Othniel Marsh thought the fossils he examined were from an animal similar to a bison.

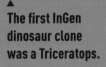

▲ The first InGen dinosaur clone was a Triceratops.

◄ This Triceratops skull was one of the largest in John Lockwood's fossil collection.

◄ Visitors at Jurassic World could see Triceratops herds up close in Gyrosphere Valley.

Fossilized Poop

Dinosaurs lived large. The biggest species could devour incredibly vast amounts of prey or plants in a single feeding session. The end result of all those supersized meals? You guessed it: poop. Dinosaurs produced huge quantities. In fact, scientists believe that the biggest plant-eating dinosaurs may have produced more than 2,000 pounds of poop every day!

Most dinosaur poop disintegrated quickly—and sources suggest that it may also have been consumed by prehistoric cockroaches. Some of it, though, has survived in fossilized form. Paleontologists have discovered petrified poop everywhere from England and Europe to the Americas, and from Asia to Africa. These fossils are called coprolites. They prove that millions of years ago, just like today, what goes in must come out!

The biggest coprolite ever found was discovered in Saskatchewan, Canada. The massive mound is 17 inches long and nearly 7 inches wide. Scientists believe that a *Tyrannosaurus rex* was probably responsible for this impressive specimen.

| 1 | 2 | 3 | 4 | 5 | 6 | 7 | 8 | 9 | 10 | 11 | 12 | 13 | 14 | 15 | 16 |

A coprolite is not actual poop. These trace fossils are petrified, which means that the original poop was replaced by minerals over time.

ONLY AT JURASSIC WORLD

◀ If this pile of poop that Owen came across became fossilized, it would be a coprolite.

Even marine reptiles like Mosasaurus have ▼ left coprolites!

"Coprolite" was named by William Buckland of England. It means "dung stone."

T. rex Fossils

First discovered: 1902

Discovered by: Barnum Brown

Location: Montana, United States

Contents of discovery: Partial skeleton

Named by: Henry F. Osborn

Name meaning: *Tyrannosaurus rex* means "king of the tyrant lizards"

The largest *T. rex* skull fossil ever found was more than 5 feet long and 3 feet wide. That's the size of a refrigerator! *T. rex*'s huge head was packed with razor-sharp teeth—as many as 60 at a time—that could grow to almost 12 inches long.

With about 50 banana-sized serrated teeth, the *T. rex* could easily tear apart meat.

Large olfactory bulbs (which are tied to sense of smell) show that the *T. rex* could sniff out most of its meals.

About fifty *T. rex* skeletons have been discovered.

A Skeleton Named Sue

A *Tyrannosaurus rex* skeleton named "Sue" is one of the coolest fossil skeletons ever found. It is about 90 percent complete—one of the most complete *T. rex* skeletons in existence. The fossil, which has a 600-pound skull, was discovered in 1990 in South Dakota. Today, this mighty specimen stands on permanent display at the Field Museum of Natural History in Chicago, Illinois.

Paleontologists have determined that the long tail of the *T. rex* was used for balance.

◄ This *T. rex* at Jurassic World let out a victorious roar after defeating a Carnotaurus.

◄ *T. rex* could bite with 10 times more force than an alligator.

◄ Owen got an up-close look at this *T. rex*'s large eye. *T. rex* are estimated to have weighed up to 20.4 tons— more than 200 times heavier than the average man.

The Bone Wars

Othniel Charles Marsh

October 29, 1831–March 18, 1899

Birthplace: Lockport, New York, United States

Mary lived: 1799–1847

Birthplace: England

Major Discovery: During his longtime rivalry with Edward Cope, which has been called the Bone Wars, he discovered 80 species of dinosaurs, including the first Pterodactyl. He named the Stegosaurus, Triceratops, Allosaurus, and more.

Other accomplishments: He was the first vertebrate paleontology professor in the United States. He also named the Brontosaurus, which is no longer recognized as its own species and is instead now known as an Apatosaurus.

Marsh named Stegosaurus, among others.

Edward Drinker Cope

July 28, 1840–April 12, 1897

Birthplace: Philadelphia, Pennsylvania, United States

Major Discovery: Cope is credited with the discovery of about 1,000 extinct species.

Other accomplishments: Fueled by his thirty-year rivalry with Marsh to discover the most dinosaurs, he amassed a collection of 13,000 bones, some of which are still on view at the American Museum of Natural History.

JURASSIC WORLD PROFILE:
DOCTOR WU

Dr. Wu is a geneticist with a long history at Jurassic World, starting in the mid-1980s. Since then, he has had a significant role in the development of the Jurassic World dinosaurs. Dr. Wu was the lead geneticist on the team that created the first dinosaurs on the island.

One of the biggest scientific impacts made by Dr. Wu was his creation of two new, hybrid dinosaurs: *Indominus rex* and Indoraptor. According to Dr. Wu, these hybrid dinosaurs could be unpredictable and dangerous because they were genetically modified using DNA from predators like the Velociraptor and *Tyrannosaurus rex*. This hypothesis was proved true.

▲ Dr. Wu's motives were honest in the beginning of his career, but by the time Jurassic World opened, some people were concerned that he'd become corrupt.

ONLY AT JURASSIC WORLD

◄ *Indominus rex* was a fierce predator, with DNA from a *T. rex*, Velociraptor, and other prehistoric animals.

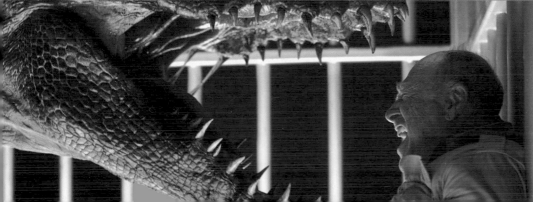

◄ The Indoraptor was Dr. Wu's most dangerous creation.

Fossil Digs

A site where paleontologists actively look for fossils is called a dig. The location of a dig depends on what a scientist hopes to find. If you're looking for *T. rex* remains, for example, you would aim your shovel at the western United States and Canada. For birdlike Oviraptor fossils, Mongolia's Gobi Desert would be a better bet. Whatever the region, places where rocks have been opened or exposed are good areas to start searching for fossils.

Extracting fossils is a long, painstaking process. First, paleontologists protect the dig site with a tent. Then they use special tools to chip the fossil out of the surrounding rock. They work slowly and carefully to avoid damaging the fossil.

Completely excavating a dig site can take weeks or even months, and it requires years of training and special tools. Workers must be able to sense how hard or soft the rock feels beneath their tools and be careful not to damage specimens—and they have to know how to make repairs if damage is done. A specimen as small as a human hand can require a year of work to expose.

Paleontologist Tools

Rock hammer: for breaking apart rock without damaging fossils

Brushes: to whisk away dirt from fossil finds

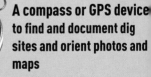

A compass or GPS device to find and document dig sites and orient photos and maps

Chisels and probes: to move away rock from the fossils

◀ Dr. Alan Grant and Dr. Ellie Sattler worked together in the field at a dig site.

Though Dr. Grant typically worked with fossils, at Jurassic Park, he learned that there was nothing quite like ▼ the real thing.

Tape measure: fossils need to be measured, as do distances between fossils

Permanent markers and plastic bags: to document and transport specimens

SPECIMEN CONTAINER

◀ This scientist worked in the field with an assortment of tools.

In the Lab

When a dig ends, another part of the paleontologist's job begins. Back in the museum or in their laboratory, or wherever they take their discoveries, scientists figure out what their newly discovered fossils mean. They compare them to older fossils and to those that other scientists have found.

Careful cleaning is a major part of this process. Cleaning can mean washing fossils with water or strong chemicals that eat away stubborn rock. It can take years to clean and sort all the fossils from a dig. However it's done, though, scientists must work very slowly to avoid breaking fragile finds or assembling pieces in the wrong order.

When the process is finally complete, paleontologists share with the scientific community the information they have gathered. They are providing new information that will help future paleontologists continue their work.

Lab work is tricky in many ways. Sometimes paleontologists find a mishmash of bones from many different animals, so they have to determine which bones belong to which animal. Sometimes it's hard to tell rock from bone, which can easily be broken.

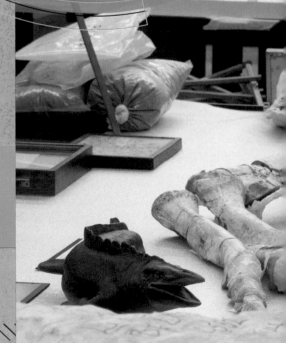

ONLY AT JURASSIC WORLD

◄ The Hammond Creation Lab at Jurassic World was one of the most technologically advanced genetics labs in the world.

One of the main focuses of the Jurassic World lab was egg production. ▼

◄ In this picture, Dr. Wu is examining a stolen specimen from the *Indominus rex*.

Paleontology

Paleontologists are scientists who are specially trained to find and study fossils. They use their skills to collect information about plants, animals (including dinosaurs), and other organisms that existed in the distant past. Paleontologists might travel all around the world to work at research sites. They might spend months or even years in a remote location searching for clues about the fossils they study. The process is long, difficult, and tiring, but it can also be exhilarating. Most paleontologists say that spending time in the field is their favorite part of the job.

While some paleontologists dig, others have different focuses. They might sketch, photograph, and document each discovery with detailed notes. They collect every scrap of information that might provide a useful clue.

Types of Paleontologists

Micropaleontology: the study of microscopic fossils, such as grains of pollen

Paleobotany: the study of fossilized plants

Paleoclimatology: the study of past climates

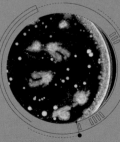

Paleoecology: the study of how fossilized organisms interacted with one another and their surroundings

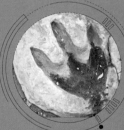

Paleoichnology: the study of trace fossils, like footprints

◀ Paleobotanists like Dr. Ellie Sattler study fossils of plant life.

Dr. Sattler was trying to learn what plant this Triceratops ate that made her sick. ▼

Taphonomy: the study of fossilization

◀ As a paleoveterinarian, Zia Rodriguez had the unique opportunity to work with living dinosaurs instead of fossils. At its peak, Jurassic World employed almost 40 paleoveterinarians.

Apatosaurus Fossils

First discovered: 1877

Discovered by: Othniel C. Marsh

Location: Como Bluff, Wyoming, United States

Contents of discovery: Partial juvenile

Named by: Othniel C. Marsh

Name meaning: *Apatosaurus* means "deceptive lizard"

Name That Dino

The name "Apatosaurus," which means "deceptive lizard," refers to this dinosaur's history of mistaken identity. Scientists first confused it with Mosasaurus, a large aquatic reptile. Later, another scientist unearthed a skeleton that he thought was a newly discovered dinosaur species, but it wasn't! It was actually an Apatosaurus skeleton lying near the skull of a different animal. The scientist named his mixed-up discovery Brontosaurus. Decades passed before paleontologists sorted out this colossal confusion.

Apatosaurus lived during the Jurassic Period, about 154 million to 150 million years ago. One of the largest animals ever to roam the Earth, Apatosaurus lumbered on four thick, strong legs. It couldn't outrun predators, but that didn't matter. Apatosaurus was so big that nothing could hurt it! This herbivore probably held its long neck and tail parallel to the ground most of the time, but it may have been able to raise its head for short periods to feast from the tallest treetops.

▲ Gyrosphere Valley offered an up-close look at the gigantic Apatosaurus.

The small skull of the Apatosaurus suggests to paleontologists that it was not intelligent.

Apatosaurus teeth functioned like a comb and were ideal for pulling leaves from trees.

Air sacs were discovered in the neck of Apatosaurus, which suggests that it was lighter than it looks!

This Apatosaurus enjoyed a delicious meal of leaves.
▼

▲ An Apatosaurus hologram greeted guests at the Jurassic World Innovation Center.

43

Major Dinosaur Discoveries

Mary Anning
The Mother of Paleontology

May 21, 1799–March 9, 1847

Birthplace: Lyme Regis, England

Major Discovery: Anning's brother discovered a strange skull around 1811, and Mary then uncovered the complete specimen. It turned out to be an extinct marine reptile, which was given the name Ichthyosaurus.

Other accomplishments: Anning uncovered a complete Plesiosaurus skeleton in 1823. She discovered Dimorphodon, the first Pterosaur outside of Germany. She also was one of the first people to study coprolites. Today, her fossils are on display at the Natural History Museum in London.

The First *T. rex*
Barnum Brown

February 12, 1873–February 5, 1963

Birthplace: Carbondale, Kansas, United States

Major Discovery: In 1902, Brown discovered the first partial *T. rex* skeleton in the Hell Creek Formation in Montana.

Other accomplishments: He also discovered Corythosaurus.

JURASSIC WORLD PROFILES:

CLAIRE DEARING

Claire Dearing, the former Director of Park Operations for Jurassic World, turned her efforts to saving the remaining dinosaurs as founder and lead organizer of the Dinosaur Protection Group (DPG). The mission of the DPG was to establish and protect the rights of all living dinosaurs. One of its main goals was to secure federal funding to continue educating the public about these incredible creatures. Claire felt responsible for what happened at Jurassic World, and she has since dedicated her life's work to saving the dinosaurs.

OWEN GRADY

Owen Grady, an animal behavior expert, spent five years training Velociraptors at Jurassic World. He joined Jurassic World in 2012 as a member of the team working on InGen's Integrated Behavioral Raptor Intelligence Study. He helped train four Velociraptors from birth and has documented his findings on film. During this training, he formed a close bond with one Velociraptor in particular, Blue.

"Do you remember the first time you saw a dinosaur? First time you see them, it's like a miracle. You read about them in books, you see the bones in museums, but you don't really believe it. They're like myths. And then you see . . . the first one alive."

—Claire Dearing

"I don't control the Raptors. It's a relationship. It's based on mutual respect."

—Owen Grady

Glossary

amber: fossilized tree resin

carnivore: an animal that eats meat

cast: a type of fossil formed when minerals and sediment fill and harden in an impression left by an organism

coprolite: fossilized poop

Cretaceous Period: The time 145 million to 65 million years ago, when dinosaurs like *Tyrannosaurus rex* lived; the third period of the Mesozoic Era

dig: an excavation conducted by a paleontology team

dinosaur: an extinct creature of the Mesozoic Era

extinct: no longer existing or living

fossil: preserved evidence of an ancient animal or plant

fossilization: the process that turns once-living organisms into fossils

herbivore: an animal that eats plants

Jurassic Period: the time 199 million to 145 million years ago; the second period of the Mesozoic Era

Mesozoic Era: the time 251 million to 65 million years ago; the period of history when dinosaurs lived

mold: an impression left by an organism that is pressed into mud and removed or decomposes

organism: a living thing, such as a plant or an animal

paleontologist: a scientist who studies organisms that lived in the distant past, mostly by examining fossils

Paleozoic Era: the time 542 million to 251 million years ago, before dinosaurs lived

Pangea: the large land mass on Earth when dinosaurs first appeared

petrified fossil: items such as bones that have turned to stone after living matter is replaced by minerals

predator: an animal that hunts and eats other animals

preserved remains: the body or parts of an organism that is trapped in amber, tar, or ice

scleral ring: a hole in the skull of an animal that encases its eyes; scleral ring size may relate to whether an animal was nocturnal

sedimentary rock: rock formed from mineral or organic matter deposited by water, ice, and wind; fossils frequently are found here

stratum: a layer of rock formed by mineral or organic matter

trace fossil: a specimen that preserves a record of an animal's activity or presence but not its body

Triassic Period: the time 251 million to 199 million years ago when dinosaurs first appeared; the first period of the Mesozoic Era

DISCOVER YOUR OWN FOSSILS!

This kit comes with two digging blocks that you can excavate, just like a real paleontologist! One digging block contains a sand tiger shark's tooth. The other contains a brachiopod, a type of marine animal. Follow these simple steps to unearth your buried treasures.

You need:

- Large sheet of white paper
- Digging blocks
- Digging tool
- Brush

Instructions:

1. Spread the paper out on a flat surface. Choose one block and place it in the center of the paper.

2. Using the digging tool, gently scrape away the clay. When you uncover part of an object, keep digging very carefully. Remove all the clay from around the object before taking it out of the block. Keep digging until you have scraped away all of the clay and are left with the pieces of your fossil.

3. Brush the objects to get rid of any extra clay. If you need to, you can also wash off the remaining clay with water to get your fossils completely clean.